54 Days on a Container Ship

54 Days on a Container Ship

Helen Murray White

Copyright © 2016 Helen Murray White
All rights reserved.

ISBN: 1537390384
ISBN 13: 9781537390383
Library of Congress Control Number: 2016914653
CreateSpace Independent Publishing Platform
North Charleston, South Carolina

This book is dedicated to the crew and officers of the *Direct Tui*, who made our voyage an unforgettable adventure. Although some of the information may have changed since we sailed, the loneliness, monotony, and danger experienced by the crew do not change with time.

Table of Contents

Chapter 1	Anticipation	1
Chapter 2	Boarding	4
Chapter 3	Loading the Containers	9
Chapter 4	Learning the Routine	14
Chapter 5	Working Men	18
Chapter 6	Are There Really Pirates?	21
Chapter 7	Suddenly, It Is Spring	24
Chapter 8	Tauranga, New Zealand	28
Chapter 9	Melbourne	36
Chapter 10	On to Sydney	45
Chapter 11	Sydney	48
Chapter 12	Change of Crew	57
Chapter 13	WDFIs	61
Chapter 14	On the Way Home	65
Chapter 15	An Unexpected Detour	71
Chapter 16	Reflections	73

About the Author 77

CHAPTER 1

Anticipation

PEOPLE CELEBRATE MILESTONES IN MANY different ways. On our twenty-fifth wedding anniversary, I told my husband that a dinner in a fine restaurant would not be a sufficient celebration. What could we do? Our daughter was in Germany studying as an American Field Service student. Why not visit her? Why not buy a Eurail pass and see all of Europe? Our answers to those questions showed our naiveté: "Yes, we'll visit Julie in Germany. We'll tour Europe in three weeks."

We visited Julie and her host family, developing a friendship with the family that has endured for thirty-plus years. We bought the Eurail pass and attempted to tour Europe in three weeks, hopping on and off the train whenever a city looked interesting. We found very quickly that our goal was impossible. Europe was much larger than we thought.

That trip, however, confirmed our love of travel and the joy of meeting new people. We traveled with only one suitcase between us and knew then that we would always go as travelers, not tourists. Meeting local residents, learning how they lived their lives, and experiencing local customs were totally impossible when staying in a luxury hotel.

When the time came to celebrate our fiftieth wedding anniversary, we had to celebrate in a most unusual fashion. No cake with punch and a receiving line for us! Why not take a cruise? Better yet, why not take a cruise on a container ship? My cousin had told us about his travels on freighter ships and encouraged us to go, but by the time we had weeks available and enough money in our pockets, freighter ships had become tramp steamers. A young couple told us about their experiences on a tramp steamer to South America—inferior accommodations and weevils in their bread. Still, we dreamed of crossing the ocean on a working ship.

We contacted freighter lines and soon received pictures of ships and their passenger cabins, routes, and ports of call. Choosing the right ship meant evaluating the number of days at sea, location of ports in the United States, and physical requirements by the line. Because Bill was approaching his seventy-fifth birthday, we could only travel on lines that would accept people under eighty. There would be no doctors on board, and participants had to prove that they were healthy and able to climb six flights of steps. We chose the Maris line and began making plans. Our doctor provided letters stating that we were in good health and able to climb the steps.

On October 18, 2004, we boarded the container ship *Direct Tui* in Long Beach, California, fulfilling our life-long dream.

The *Tui*, named after an Australian bird, sailed from Long Beach to Tauranga, New Zealand; Melbourne and Sydney, Australia; and back to Long Beach on a proposed forty-two-day voyage. Travel dates had to be flexible as there were many events that might accelerate or delay port arrival and departure times. We soon discovered how true this was. Little did we know that departure would be five days after we boarded the ship. Because there was a stevedore slowdown, the *Tui* had already unloaded some cargo in Ensenada, Mexico, and had waited five days at anchor for a berth in Long Beach. And little did we know that our return to Long Beach would be delayed because of another stevedore slow down, necessitating an unloading in San Francisco and Ensenada, Mexico. The proposed forty-two-day voyage turned into a fifty-four-day voyage.

CHAPTER 2

Boarding

THE *TUI* WAS LATE ARRIVING in Long Beach. The ship's travel agent called us. "The *Tui* is not docking today. Wait until tomorrow." Three more days passed until finally she told us, "You can board tomorrow morning, as soon as the ship docks."

It was still very dark at 6:00 a.m. when the *Tui* slowly edged into the dock. That was a comforting sight because we had already had moments of concern as we tried to find the correct commercial dock, pass through the security gate, and locate a van that would take us to the ship. Unlike cruising on a passenger line, there was no one to meet us; we were on our own. It had sounded easy, but it wasn't easy for novices who were unacquainted with ships and docks. I don't remember any real security check except for someone who glanced at our passports and motioned us toward a waiting van. A tall black man standing by the van asked where we were going.

"To the *Tui*, which is sailing to New Zealand and Australia," Bill replied.

The man seemed surprised and responded, "Mister, that's a lotta water." He was so right!

The travel agent had described this as a twenty-six-book voyage. (This was before the age of Kindles.) We were determined to travel with a small amount of luggage, which meant a personal bag for each of us and a duffel bag containing at least twenty-six books, CDs, and snacks. The van stopped alongside the ship, and the driver set our bags on the dock. We stood there, wondering what to do next. A crew member saw us, lifted the heavy duffel to his shoulder, and walked rapidly toward the ship. The bags were taken to our cabin; we only had to maneuver up the gangplank. The rungs were placed at an angle, not flat. I wasn't sure whether to place my foot on each rung or every other one. Holding the swaying rope, I stepped carefully on each rung. Later in the voyage, it was easy to step on every other rung, just as the crew members did.

The steward met us on the deck and motioned for us to follow him to the conference room, where we met the captain. He was a big, burly man with a bass voice that could make "hello" sound like a command. We shook hands. "I am the captain," he said. No more conversation because he was too busy overseeing the loading and examining paperwork connected with all the containers.

We followed the steward up more steps to F deck and entered our cabin, called the owner's cabin, located just under the bridge. It was between the captain's cabin and the chief engineer's cabin. The three cabins were the only cabins located on that deck. It looked exactly like the pictures that the freighter travel agent had sent. The cabin was the size of a small apartment, with a large sitting room complete with couch, loveseat, two occasional chairs, an office-size writing desk, file cabinet, small refrigerator, and bookshelves. The bedroom contained a queen-size bed positioned in the center of the room, accessible from both sides. A small dressing table, drawers for clothing, and a large hanging closet completed the room. Five large portholes faced forward for an unobstructed view of the containers and the ocean.

The steward, who was named Than, became our chief source of information. His duties were to care for officers and passengers. "Where are you from?" we asked.

When he replied, "Myanmar," we were puzzled. Then he said, "Burma."

Of course! I remembered Burma during World War II, when pilots flew out of Burma on their bombing runs.

Than, a most efficient steward

The crew was from Myanmar, the captain and chief officer were from Poland, and the chief engineer was from Ukraine. English was the official language spoken on board, although there were many times when we couldn't understand each other's accents. The most difficulty we had was in understanding the passengers from New Zealand. But more about them later.

Than asked, "Would you like breakfast? Ham and scrambled eggs?" Yes, we had only had coffee and a breakfast bar about 4:30 a.m. Back down to B deck where the officers' dining room was located.

Our first breakfast aboard the *Tui*

Than introduced the cook working in the galley, located between the officers' dining room and the crew's dining room. The cook, a plump young guy resembling a smiling Buddha, was resting following the preparation of meals for both dining rooms.

On that first day, the cook served a lunch of soup, baked fish, boiled potatoes, broccoli well seasoned with garlic, and honeydew melon for dessert. Potatoes were usually served in the officers' dining room; rice was served in the crew's dining room. Curry was popular on the crew side, and we were told that we could order any dish from the crew's dining room. The Myanmar cook seasoned with more spices than the Filipino cook who came on board in Sydney. Oh, how we longed for him on the return trip!

All food was basic and healthy, appropriate for men who worked long, hard hours. There were few fried meats, no gooey sauces or fancy desserts, which meant no fear of gaining extra pounds. Desserts were usually fresh fruit: apples, pears, bananas, oranges, kiwi, or melon. The one exception was on Sunday when the cook served ice cream. Coffee was always available in the dining room, with coffee and cookies at teatime, if we chose. Before dinner, the Myanmar cook put out appetizers on a separate table: salami, cold cuts, cheese, and pickled and smoked herring. For some strange reason, these delicacies disappeared on the return voyage, and no one seemed to know why.

After we ate the filling lunch and unpacked our bags, we tried to go topside to look at the harbor view but found that all exits were locked while the ship was in port. Later, we discovered why. In order to go to the bridge, we had to walk down the inside steps to A deck, walk outside and up the outside steps to F deck, then one up one more flight to the bridge. This was the reason we had to supply the ship's company with a health certificate from our doctor saying we were able to walk up and down steps! We understood the requirement and vowed to get in better condition as soon as possible. Two weeks later, despite sore leg muscles, we were able to walk up and down without being winded (at least most of the time). First Officer Thomas told us that he had had to acclimate to the steps, too—and he was a young man.

CHAPTER 3

Loading the Containers

AS RESIDENTS OF THE MIDWEST unaccustomed to commercial shipping, we watched the loading and unloading of containers with fascination. The huge overhead cranes moved along the dock on rail tracks. An operator sat inside a cab suspended from the crane, about one hundred feet in the air. Below him were cables and a lift with four clamps, which he positioned over the container corners. With a snap (or sometimes a bang) and a jar, the container was connected, lifted up, and placed on the bed of a waiting truck or lowered into position on the ship. The operator made this precise connection and lowered the container in no more than thirty seconds. He was in a sitting position but had to lean forward and look down continuously. Because of the stress involved, the operators worked short hours, taking frequent breaks.

If the containers were not taken to their destinations, they were placed in carefully arranged stacks in the storage area. From the bridge, we saw a panoply of colors: red, white, blue, and green containers, stacked like little matchboxes against the green California hills.

By Tuesday morning, the operators had removed many more containers and toward the bow sat a large twin-screw powerboat tied securely to a container. Men were climbing around the boat making ready to unload it. The lift was lowered to the dock where a "boat spreader" with slings was attached. It was lowered over the boat and more men appeared to attach the slings under the boat. The boat was lifted in the air and moved very slowly over the side of the ship, and placed in the water. The vessel-assist boat came alongside and discharged the owner and mate, who boarded the powerboat, started the engine, and pulled out of the slings. The captain later told us that the boat was a Riviera, which cost a million dollars, cheaper to buy in Australia and transport it to the United States.

Later, three semitrailers carrying fifth-wheel RV campers pulled up. Each RV was secured to a container bottom and lowered into the hold. They were followed by a machine manufactured in Caldwell, Idaho, which had *mulching* written on the side.

One of the RVs being loaded

The next surprise was when the crane operator lifted the deck cover and set it on the dock. Looking down from our portholes, we saw containers stacked six deep in the hold below the main deck. After the covers were replaced, containers could be stacked six high on the deck. I was so amazed by the precise placement of the containers. None had to be moved to another location, either during loading or later during unloading; they were taken off in the same sequence as they had been placed on the ship. I asked Captain Peter how the operators knew which container to place either below deck or on the deck. His response was direct: "It can only be done with computers."

Captain Kleszewski (Captain Peter) talked with us and apologized for having no time to say more than hello the day before. He told us that the *Tui*, considered a small container vessel, could carry as many as 2200 containers but carried only 1700 on the trip to California. The cargo was always more valuable than the ship. The *Tui* was valued at $38 million, but the cargo was valued at $80 million. One container of frozen shrimp could be worth $1 million. Containers carried everything imaginable, from small objects such as records and CDs to precious items for museum exhibits.

Tuesday evening, we were joined by fellow passenger Rob, who was returning to New Zealand after visiting his brother in Los Angeles. We had communication problems immediately. Rob said that he missed eating fresh "veegies" when in California because his brother stopped for fast-food lunches every day. He said *seeven* for *seven*, *goy* for *guy* and something strange for a long *a* vowel sound. The vowel changes, plus his rapid, staccato speech caused us to frequently ask, "What?" But Rob had as much trouble understanding us as we had understanding him. The horse grooms who boarded in Tauranga and Sydney had the same pattern of speech. We found Kiwis (as they call themselves) more difficult to understand than Aussies.

Friday morning, we were awakened by the engine's vibration and the ship's movement. At around 6:45 a.m., the ship was headed to sea beneath a beautiful pink sunrise surrounded by a baby-blue sky. Catalina Island came into view on the right. We passed the Coronado Islands, and after that, we saw no land for two weeks. Once the ship was out of port, exits were opened. We walked up one flight to the bridge where the duty officer saw us, invited us inside, and pointed out the operating systems. The ship was on autopilot, with monitors indicating directions, water depth, wind speed, and any problems in the holds. He welcomed us to come to the bridge at any time, except when the ship was in port or escorted into a harbor with the pilot on board. This rule was relaxed later in the trip.

    The sea was calm, and the ship swayed gently from side to side. The dark indigo blue of the water was in contrast to the bright red and creamy yellow of the superstructure. Astern, the dark-blue sea changed to turquoise with white foam in the following wake. Than put deck chairs under the sheltered bridge on our deck which provided protection from the sun. F deck became our own private deck.

Our own private deck

CHAPTER 4

Learning the Routine

WHEN WE TOLD FRIENDS ABOUT our travel plans, they said, "You're going to do WHAT?" The second question was "What are you going to DO all day?" Contrary to their concerns, we had no difficulty falling into the daily routine on board ship. The days passed quickly. Bill read constantly, going through all those twenty-six books we had packed. I read too, kept a diary, and practiced drawing and yoga.

There were many opportunities for exercise. In addition to all those trips up and down the steps for meals, two times around the main deck was equal to a half mile. Even though we had to balance ourselves with the rolling of the ship, I felt more buoyant than when walking on solid ground. The most enjoyable experience was to be on deck, looking at the constantly changing colors and shapes of the sky, clouds, and water—an experience that cannot be described in words. It can only be seen and felt.

Saturdays were reserved for emergency drills. Since the primary purpose was to train the crew, the drill was more involved than standing around in a life jacket, as I'd done on cruise ships. We were told to listen for the general alarm—seven short blasts and one long blast—grab life jackets and proceed to the nearest assembly point.

The desk in our room

I spent a lot of time writing

As soon as we heard the blasts, we donned our life jackets and helmets and walked quickly down the inside steps to deck A, then down another flight to the main deck where we assembled at the stern muster station. The crew was divided into two groups, with passengers following the first officer to the lifeboat. The first mate told us to get inside the lifeboat, but Rob refused to enter. As the only woman on board, I felt that I must keep up with the men. I willed myself to NOT feel claustrophobic, but it was difficult since there was no ventilation on the inside of the lifeboat. We all took off our life jackets and fastened our seat belts as we sat on narrow benches going around all sides of the boat. Second Officer Kyaw demonstrated the lifesaving equipment on board and asked the crew member responsible for operating the boat to go through throttle positions. He explained that in case of emergency, the boat would be lowered into the water with crew and passengers inside. His description made it all sound very normal, and I thought I could handle that, but a later training film showed the lifeboat shooting into the water like a missile.

After that exercise, the group moved to where the life raft was located. The raft was enclosed in a fiberglass tube that opened automatically and inflated when the raft hits the water. There were limited supplies on board the raft: water, food, a tarp to catch rainwater, fishing gear, flares. Chief Officer Karaskiewicz instructed us to drink no water the first day, and only a half liter of water the day after that. As an aside, he said to me, "Don't expect to catch any fish out here. The water is too deep." These exercises didn't make me feel any safer, but they did give me more respect for the perils of the sea. My feelings were closer to Rob's. As he expressed it, "If anything happens, oy'll take me chances."

Sundays were generally a day of rest for the crew. As we walked around the deck and up and down the steps, everything was quiet. The ship seemed deserted. Occasionally we saw a Myanmar crew member relaxing in his sarong or heard laughter in the TV room. On the first Sunday out, the captain was sunbathing on the deck outside his cabin. The only crew members who appeared to be on duty were the cook, the steward, and the officer on the bridge. Thanks to modern science, only the engines and navigation systems were working.

CHAPTER 5

Working Men

A_LTHOUGH THE_ *Tui* WAS A working ship, it was remarkably clean. The day after leaving port, the crew used power hoses to wash away diesel residue on the decks.

Two of the Myanmar crew members

Everyone removed deck shoes when going into the cabins, preventing oil stains on the carpets. Our cabin was cleaned daily—Than scrubbed the bathroom floor and vacuumed the carpet. Our requests to replace a light bulb or repair the shower drain were answered promptly. We felt the crew was determined to provide us with a good sailing experience, although their first obligation was to move the ship from port to port as quickly as possible. The captain said, "We are only making money when we are sailing."

This statement represents a dilemma in the shipping industry today. There is a worldwide slowdown of stevedores in developed countries. The worst slowdown is in the US ports, which was what caused the delay in Long Beach. Crane operators make about $16,000 a month; stevedores make $8,000, paid by the hour. Their unions are asking for more employees to get the jobs done. Dock operators are resisting because that would cut into their profits. In contrast, crane operators in Singapore are paid by container moved, so they are motivated to move quickly. Slowdowns can also occur because of weather problems. When we were in Sydney, the ship was in port for four days, but for two days, gusty winds set off wind alarms and shut down the cranes until the winds subsided. Whatever the reason for slowing down, the captains, ship owners, and transport companies must wait until the crane operators and stevedores have done their jobs, no matter how long it takes.

Bill asked Chief Engineer Zoroyan, "Would it be possible to see the engine room?"

"But of course," he said.

We followed him down to deck A and then down more steps where we donned helmets and earplugs before entering a cavernous area containing four huge generators, two large turbines, the propeller shaft, and thousands of electrical wires. Normally only two generators operate at one time: one for the ship's functions, the other to power refrigerated containers (capacity three hundred on this ship). On the return trip from New Zealand, the ship carried 268 containers of frozen food; the crew constantly had to monitor the temperature. It seemed that Chief Electrician Pascale was always on call. He would be eating his meal, get a call, and suddenly jump up to run and monitor the frozen food.

CHAPTER 6

Are There Really Pirates?

THE SUN WAS BRIGHT, AND a warm breeze was blowing in the passageway. As I walked toward the outside deck, I saw First Officer Karaskiewicz cleaning out a locker. He placed a booklet on the deck: *Pirates and Armed Robbers: A Master's Guide.* I was startled by the title because my knowledge of pirates was limited to the swashbuckling Blackbeard of the 1700s or the Johnny Depp movie, *Pirates of the Caribbean.* I asked, "Are there really pirates?"

The first officer answered, "Yes, there are pirates, particularly around the coast of West Africa, Indonesia, and the Philippines." The booklet instructed the ship's master on how to prevent and handle raids. Bill and I later observed the crew's practice pirate drill. There were no guns or ammunition on board; their only defense was the ship's ability to outrun the pirates, shooting water at their boats with high-pressure water hoses.

The pirates ranged from the poor raiding ships for money to organized crime rings to international groups bent on stealing a ship. The International Transport Workers Federation reported an escalation of attacks to more than 2,635 in the past decade. Not only are the attacks increasing in number but also in ferocity. Two vessels were attacked in the Straits of Malacca (Indonesia) and were left sailing with no one on the bridge. Pirates took the navigating officers below while they raided for money and valuables. Both vessels were oil tankers; a collision could have caused a major environmental catastrophe.

First Officer Thomas said to me, "If they board and want your gold wedding ring, give it to them. They won't hesitate to cut off your finger."

Countries such as Indonesia and Brazil and regions like West Africa lack the resources to monitor their coastlines or capture and prosecute the criminals. Thus, they are havens for pirate groups. Naturally political and economic conditions in these areas are also factors. NUMAST, then the British maritime professionals' union, has been battling for international cooperation to solve the problem.

In 2006, NUMAST joined with the Dutch union FWZ, and they changed their name to Nautilus International. Their goal is to work together to decrease the dangers from pirates operating along the coasts of West Africa, Somalia, Indonesia, India, and Tasmania. The union has been working with those governments to increase protection for seafarers as well as provide extra compensation for those sailing in these dangerous areas. They are also protecting the rights of seamen who refuse to sail in these waters. That applies only to members of the Nautilus International Union. Those seafarers working on ships sailing under flags of convenience do not have these protections.

Another important precaution was to lock all outside exits when entering or leaving a port. When the ship was in port, there was only one exit left unlocked, located on A deck. That was why we had to walk down inside steps and walk up the outside steps on that first day we were on board. The locked doors also prevent stowaways, and the crew maintains constant vigilance to prevent them from boarding the ship.

Captain Behr (who boarded the ship in Sydney) said, "I've found stowaways on, between, and *in* containers, not always alive." He also told us that on one trip to North Africa, five stowaways slipped onto the ship. They weren't found until the ship was at sea. He immediately had them locked in one of the ship's cabins and then tried to leave them in French or Dutch ports. Neither country would accept them. After the ship returned to its home port in Germany, policemen escorted the five—shackled hand and foot—and flew them back to their home country at a cost of 40,000 German marks. Captain Behr said, "I have told the company that I do not want to captain a ship that goes to Africa."

CHAPTER 7

Suddenly, It Is Spring

Wednesday morning, Chief Officer Karaskiewicz (it was easier to call him by his first name, Thomas), announced, "At 2200 this evening, we will cross the equator." Just before 10:00 p.m., we walked up the inside steps to the bridge and opened the door. It took a few minutes for our eyes to adjust to the darkness before we saw the red-and-green lights of the operating systems.

Second Officer Kyaw said, "You are now crossing the equator." I remembered the red line indicating the equator that was always present on our school globes and jokingly asked, "Yes, but where is the red line?" Rob, Officer Kyaw, and the two of us watched as the ship ploughed ahead through the black water, the outlines of the ship and containers delineated by the ship's forward light and a large moon behind intermittent clouds. We were in the Southern Hemisphere. It was spring, not fall!

The next morning Captain Peter gave us equatorial baptism certificates signed by Neptune and witnessed by Captain Kleszewski, stating that we had been "cleaned from dust and dirt of land masses" and baptized to sail on all waters north and south of the equator. Bill's baptismal name was Rigel, and mine was Bellatrix, two of the brightest stars in the Orion constellation.

At breakfast, Chief Officer Thomas said, "Tomorrow we will cross the International Date Line. There will be no Friday this week." I had just read Umberto Eco's book *The Island of the Day Before*, set in the seventeenth century when navigators and astronomers were trying to understand longitude and determine which country would be home to the prime meridian. The priest in that book had clocks set for different time zones all around the world. Imagine the ticking of all those clocks! Emotionally it didn't feel right to lose a day, although I knew we'd find that day on our return to California. In fact, it felt worse on the return trip. There is something psychologically disturbing about repeating a day that you have just lived through.

Thursday was a Myanmar holiday. The crew rested. According to their tradition, when there was a full moon, a god left the moon and came to earth. That called for a party the next day—Saturday.

Time for a party

The party was located on E deck, the deck just below ours. I looked over our outside deck and saw colored lights strung from railings and tables and benches set up with the cook lighting charcoal in a barbeque brazier. When we stepped onto E deck, we were greeted with smiles and toasts. Bowls of spicy cashews, wontons, small meatballs, and Indonesian fish chips had been placed on the tables for early snacking. The cook made a huge bowl of fried noodles and barbequed many kinds of meats: pork chops, chicken hearts on skewers, chicken breasts, beef, fish, squid, and sausages. He must have emptied all the food in his freezer!

Enjoying the party with Rob, Captain Peter, and Engineer Zoroyan

Drizzly rain fell briefly, but it was not enough to dampen the spirits. One crew member, trying to be hospitable, kept offering us more food and drinks until an officer had another crew member put him to bed. Second Officer Kyaw apologized and said, "It is not our way to become drunk." We told him that we were not offended. These men had been at sea for several months and needed a change in their daily routine. Many bottles of Johnny Walker and many bottles of beer were consumed, but the crew knew that they must stay within limits. Unfortunately, fellow passenger Rob didn't know his limits. He didn't come to breakfast the following morning and stayed in his cabin for two days after the party.

As we sat at the table talking with the captain and officers, a perfectly full moon rose over the stern, its light creating a silver path in the black water. The rain was over; the air was warm.

CHAPTER 8

Tauranga, New Zealand

THE FIRST PORT OF CALL was Tauranga, New Zealand. Officer Thomas said, "Get up early in the morning; the view is beautiful." At 5:30 a.m., we felt that the ship was barely moving. Putting our clothes on hurriedly, we dashed to the bridge. The sun was just breaking through. There was a bright light directly ahead, about halfway up a mountain. Small islands began popping into view, some cone shaped, some flat on top, some round. Clouds hung over distant mountain ranges as if secured there.

The ship slowed for the harbor pilot to board and guide it into port. Marker buoys were placed to the right of the mountain, which was located dead ahead. What had appeared to be a large island was Mount Maunganui, located on the tip of a peninsula. The *Tui* entered a horseshoe-shaped harbor, the mount and a large resort area on the left, and docks for commercial ships on the right. Once inside the harbor, the ship started turning in what seemed to be a very small area for a large ship. With little tugs pushing, the pilot steered us through a 180-degree turn. Now the *Tui* was turned with the bow facing Mount Maunganui and the mouth of the harbor.

54 Days on a Container Ship

View of Mount Maunganui

Tug pushing our ship into place

We were quickly cleared by customs and told that we could leave the ship for the day. "Be back by seven p.m. The ship sails at nine thirty," instructed the captain. On a working boat, a ship does not wait for tardy passengers, and to be safe, we returned by five.

A yellow line led away from the dock to a van, which shuttled us to the security gate. From there, it was a short walk into the city. Tauranga is a clean, quiet city with buildings clustered around the harbor area. The street closest to the water is called the Strand, and it is home to a continuous string of bars and restaurants, all trying to attract customers. We dined in the sun, enjoying the blue water, many sailboats, and bright-green hills in the distance, thinking how different this was from Missouri, where the temperature was thirty-four degrees Fahrenheit.

Bar on the Strand

After we returned to the ship for dinner, we met two new passengers in the dining room. One was the company supervisor, and in honor of the occasion, we were served steak with béarnaise sauce, French fries, salad, and red wine. The supervisor was a young man in his early forties whose responsibility was to inspect ships for the Rickmers Reederei company and troubleshoot any problems. He stayed on the ship until we reached Sydney, and we had many interesting conversations with him about his travel experiences and his views about the world's economies. He told friends in Australia to learn Mandarin Chinese because China would become their natural trading partner in years to come.

The second passenger was a groom accompanying six horses from Tauranga to Melbourne. (Our first fellow passenger, Rob, had reached his destination and departed.) The groom was a small, wiry man with not an extra ounce of fat on his body, blue eyes, and receding but still wavy gray hair. He looked to be in his early sixties but may have been younger than he appeared. A lifetime of hard work was apparent in his rough hands. He wasn't sure how these horses would travel because they had never been away from their farm before. Their owner was sending them to Tasmania for training at a cost of $2500 each for their passage.

We wanted to see how the horses traveled, so we walked down to the main deck where they were stabled in six individual stalls within a container. They appeared to be happily munching their grain, but Kevin (Keevin, as he introduced himself) said they weren't drinking because the water tasted different.

The ship was on the move the following morning, and we watched the New Zealand coast as we rounded the tip of North Island. Sailboats of all sizes dotted the coastline. The mountains were very rugged; some had little vegetation. Their sides plunged directly into the ocean, with foamy breakers crashing against them. On the western side, the beaches were golden sand; now and then there were large, mounded dunes similar to those seen along the Oregon coast. The clouds above reflected the same brownish gold on their undersides as the gold sandy beaches below them. Kevin said, "These waters are great for fishing, and they are also breeding grounds for the great white sharks."

Kevin and his horses

New Zealanders have named the two main islands that make up their country North Island and South Island, perhaps because each island is different in climate and topography. While North Island has sandy beaches and is a popular area for swimming, boating, and water sports, South Island has a cooler climate with snow on the high mountains, glaciers, and fiords. It is a popular place for winter sports.

When our ship was off the New Zealand cost, the weather was perfect for deck sitting and for walking around the main deck. We walked to the bow—and stopped—it was amazingly quiet. The sea was perfectly calm; there was no engine noise, only the soft slush of water against the ship. It was as quiet as sailing on a sailboat. Off to starboard were the Hen and Chickens Islands, the last visible islands of New Zealand. We sat on the chocks, breathing the fresh, salty air, listening to the soft "shush" of the water, and recalling all the good times we have had on the water.

From our first fourteen-foot outboard boat to weekends spent on the muddy Mississippi River to vacations on Long Island Sound, we had never tired of being on water. Later cruises in the Caribbean and up the inland waterway to Alaska had whetted our appetites for the sea. And now—the very best of all—we had many, many days to absorb the beauty of the ocean.

Typical sight of following wake

There was a period of rolling water, rain, and cool temperatures as we crossed the Tasman Sea, but by morning, the sea was calm again.

Officer Thomas had warned us that the Tasman Sea was frequently rough, but on this trip, it behaved itself.

As the ship approached Melbourne, a pilot boat came alongside and discharged the harbor captain. These captains have to be in good physical shape, able to jump from the pilot boat to the hanging ladder and then to climb up to the main deck of the ship. It's not an easy task when there are waves and rolling waters. Bill talked with one harbor captain who said the job was not easy, but it meant that he could be home with his family rather than be away several months on a cruise. The harbor captains always guide incoming ships because they know the harbor waters and dangerous tides.

A narrow channel was ahead, the changes in the color of the water identifying the shallow water outside the line of buoys. A lighthouse and beach were on the right; a promontory was on the left. Buoy markers were white, and sea gulls rested on them, but no seals were in the hut built especially for them to rest. It was only a wooden platform with a roof. Maybe the seals did not like it. The marked channel looked wide enough for only one ship; however, a larger ship carrying 4100 containers overtook the *Tui*. That ship already had a berth and was speeding toward it. We would have to remain at anchor outside the harbor until a berth was available. The *Tui* couldn't dock that evening, but when Bill and I walked on the deck, we could see the Melbourne skyline in the distance.

CHAPTER 9

Melbourne

~~~~

MELBOURNE—THE OFFICIAL TOURIST GUIDEBOOK CALLS it one of the world's most livable cities. It is cosmopolitan, and the residents are warm and friendly. There is an ethnic mix, and overall it has the feeling of London. The city bustles with celebrations in the springtime, the most important being the Spring Racing Carnival. From October until mid-November, jockeys and thoroughbreds from all over Australia come to Melbourne. Women shop for exclusive new outfits; visitors arrive from England. A whirl of parties, champagne, and balls culminates with the Emirates Melbourne Cup. (We had earlier listened to the racing of the Melbourne Cup on our shortwave radio.)

Another interesting item we heard on the shortwave radio was the announcement of George Bush's reelection as president. The radio announcer said, "Can you believe that the people of America put that moron back in the White House?" I suppose it illustrated that people around the world had opinions about American elections.

Melbourne, settled along the harbor and the Yarra River in 1835, is laid out in a rectangular pattern with wide streets and short blocks. It's very easy for a tourist to get around, and to encourage tourism, the city runs a free tourist tram called the City Circle. The tram travels through all the downtown, stopping at historic sites and civic attractions.

Our first stop was at the famous Queen Victoria Market. It's similar to the big city market in Guadalajara, Mexico, although much cleaner. We always like to visit markets in every country, looking to see what kinds of food are available. Here, there were many meat stalls with cuts of lamb, beef, and kangaroo. The kangaroo meat was dark red and looked like solid muscle—no fat. I read that the absence of fat makes it a very healthy meat. Deli products from every country around the world were available. Also there were many kinds of fish I had never seen before, plus an abundance of fresh fruits and vegetables.

After we were finished in the market, we took a short walk down the hill toward center city. Black suits for both men and women seemed to be the business dress code, as it had been in New Zealand. Everyone seemed more formally dressed than in the United States. Another immediate impression was that there were so few fat people. Could it be the emphasis on exercise and the absence of fast-food restaurants?

Bourke Street Mall, a walking street, was home to a large retail shopping area and the Myer department store, reminiscent of our grand old department stores in the United States. It was decorated for Christmas, with spring outfits in the windows. Clerks wanted to talk with us when they discovered we were from the United States. They were in no hurry—they asked questions, and we made small purchases.

The store occupied a block on Bourke Street and the block behind it on Lonsdale Street. Bill sat on a park bench while I searched for paper goods. I was almost lost before I found my way back to Bourke Street and Bill, who was still patiently waiting. A little later, while walking on Little Bourke Street, we saw familiar faces. Three Myanmar crew members—the second engineer, the fitter, and the oiler—were buying gifts to take home to their families.

We had been told to get off the tram at Spencer Street and walk a few blocks to Little Collins Street, where the Seafarers' Mission was located.

The Seafarers' Center

A van was available there to transport seamen to their ships with no charge. The same courtesy was extended to us as passengers on a working ship. When we walked into the Seafarers' Mission, we saw those three familiar faces again. The men had completed their shopping and were waiting for the shuttle, too. They insisted on buying us a drink, then another. Bill wanted to buy them a drink, but no. They said, "It is our custom to be hospitable."

Their English was limited, but we exchanged information about our countries. Myanmar is controlled by a military government, which negotiates contracts between ship owners and employees. One young man said, "We call our government the Mafia because they have guns and tell us what to do." I felt sad to learn that these kind, gentle people were ruled by guns. A volunteer later told us that seamen were frequently placed on flags-of-convenience ships, on which working conditions are deplorable. There was no recourse for these seamen.

The next day was beautiful and sunny, warmer than the day before. The tram was crowded with tourists and locals. We decided to get off at Russell Street and visit the Old Melbourne Gaol. It was the first jail built in Melbourne and was the site of 136 hangings. The building, constructed of native bluestone, had three levels, cells opening on a main hall, with catwalks above, similar to many historic prison configurations in the United States. In the 1800s, authorities felt that severe punishment would make inmates reform. When inmates were taken to the yard, the jailers made them wear cloth masks and covered their hands with wooden paddles resembling ping-pong paddles. No one could be identified, and each prisoner suffered total isolation inside his (or her) own five-by-eight-foot concrete cell with no heat. The only daylight came through a small window covered with opaque glass and positioned almost at the ceiling. Doors were made of heavy steel with only a peephole for the guards to see the prisoners and an opening where the prisoners placed their hands to receive food.

Current cells contained exhibits relating to the old jail, and some had death masks on display. Because phrenology was popular in that era, death masks were made of the condemned men and woman so doctors could study their skulls and see if lumps and bumps could determine the source of their criminal behavior.

Inside the Old Melbourne Gaol

Other cells told stories of famous criminals. Their histories outlined the history of Australia: conflict with the Aborigines, slum conditions where poor immigrants lived, alcohol and opium abuse, the gold rush, and fights in the bush country. The first man hanged was an Aborigine—later there were Asians, Indians, Irish, and even an African American descended from a slave. The most famous outlaw hanged there was Ned Kelly, a poor Irishman from the bush who started as a thief and ended as a murderer.

Ned Kelly's father was one of the poor souls emptied from England's prisons and sent to Australia after being convicted of the theft of two pigs. Ned's father, Red, and Ned's mother, Ellen, eked out a minimal living in an area north of Melbourne where Red supplemented the family's income by stealing horses. After Red was convicted and sentenced to jail in Melbourne, Ned took over as the family's breadwinner, working as a timber cutter, fencer, and cattle herder. What he really wanted was to become a bushranger—an outlaw living in the wild Australian countryside. Ned put together a gang, and they hid out at the head of King River, a location that was mountainous, full of gullies and hiding places. Locals informed Ned when anyone unknown was entering the area.

Because Ned and his gang were in danger of being cornered by the police, he designed suits of armor for them to wear during a shootout. The newly passed Felons Apprehension Act permitted the shooting of bushrangers on sight without the protection of arrest or trial. The pictures of Ned wearing his armor and the story of his life came to symbolize a fight for justice and liberty for innocent people. Ned came to represent the lives of all the poor Irish who had been sent to Australia to survive against unspeakable odds. His story captivated writers and moviemakers, and Ned became one of Australia's folk heroes. American moviegoers may remember the movie *Ned Kelly*, starring Mick Jagger.

We spent almost two hours touring the jail and talking with the docent, who spun story after story about the prison. As we were leaving, a group of primary-school children entered the building wearing their school uniforms and Tilley hats. The docent told the story of Ned Kelly and pointed to the platform where Kelly had stood just before the noose was placed around his neck. Ned's last words were said to be these: "Such is life." What a contrast between these clean-looking young people and those prisoners who were made invisible in this place.

Our next stop was the Greek area of Melbourne, located on Lonsdale Street and said to be the largest Greek settlement outside of Greece. Restaurants, boutiques, and travel agencies were decorated with blue and white, the Greek national colors. We found a restaurant with a menu we liked: moussaka, kabobs, and baklava for dessert.

Then it was back on the tram to the next stop—the parliament building and, across the street, the Windsor Hotel. It was a short walk from there to both the Treasury Gardens and the Fitzroy Gardens, where Captain Cook's house was located.

Captain Cook's cottage

Captain Cook's cottage, originally built by his parents in 1752, was dismantled brick by brick, shipped from England, and put back together on its present site in 1934. Visitors may go through the house and wander in the garden, which is filled with plants that would have been found in an eighteenth-century British garden. Captain Cook required his crew to eat local vegetation—spinach, for example, was introduced to England by Cook. Cook's crew did not get scurvy, the cause of death for many seafarers in the 1700s. I noted that Captain

Cook sailed into Botany Bay, the port in Sydney where our ship was scheduled to arrive.

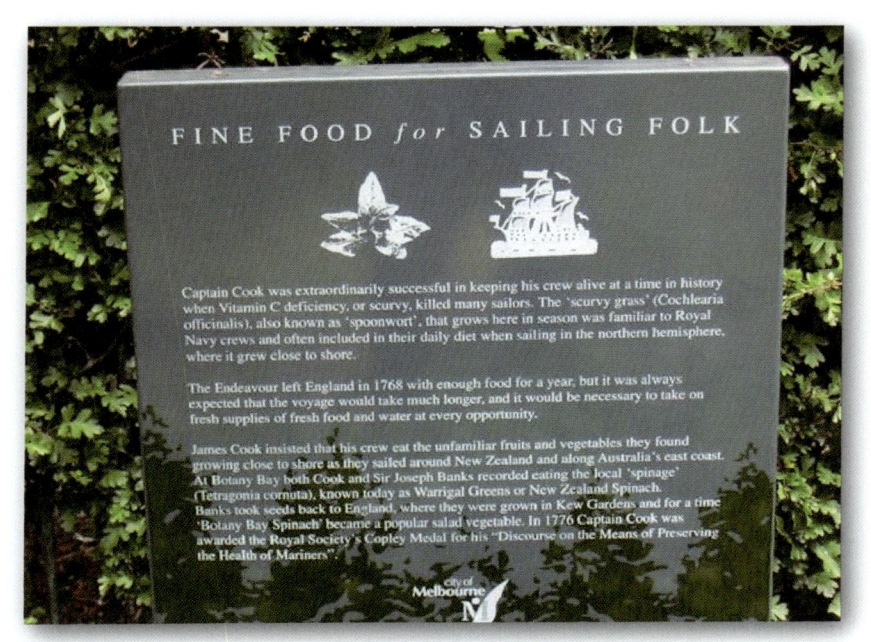

Food for Cook's crew

There were so many more sights to see but not enough time—the day was over. We made our way back to the Stella Maris Seafarers' Mission. While waiting for the van, we talked with one of the mission's volunteers. He told us about Australia's kangaroos. The small ones are called *wallabies*; the *grays* are five to six feet tall and the *big reds* are over six feet tall. The volunteer told us that he played golf on the outskirts of Melbourne and frequently saw kangaroos watching as he drove the ball.

"No problem," he said, "as long as you leave them alone." He continued, "Everyone thinks that they are cute and cuddly, but they can tear you apart if they are angry."

The following morning, the captain told us that the ship would not leave until 2:00 p.m., and we could have another day in Melbourne. Because a light rain was falling and we had planned to visit the Docklands, which involved a lot of outdoor walking, we decided to stay on board. Melbourne has extensive building plans for the Docklands. The city is reclaiming land around the old dock area and building high-rise apartments, large office complexes, a soccer stadium, private marinas, walking paths, and parks. Plans are for twenty thousand people to live there with twenty-five thousand more jobs. A one-bedroom apartment was selling for $350,000; a two-bedroom apartment was $450,000 and a penthouse was going for $1 million. (For reference, the Australian dollar was then valued at seventy-five cents to the American dollar.) Three-quarters of the apartments were purchased for investments, not private ownership. This information was given to us by a taxi driver who was very proud of his country and the current government. He told us that Australia had one of the highest standards of living in the world.

CHAPTER 10

On to Sydney

LEAVING MELBOURNE AROUND EIGHT THIRTY on a rainy evening, we sailed under the West Gate Bridge, the lights illuminating what seemed to be little clearance above or to the starboard side. The trip to Sydney would take a day and a night, and we were told to watch for whales. We saw only a school of porpoise, but the time gave us an opportunity to talk with the new captain, taking over command in Sydney. He was German, lived in a little village near Hamburg and he seemed surprised to learn that we knew the area and had friends living in Luneburg. Captain Behr was about five foot ten inches tall, age 57, with dark brown hair (what was left of it), a beard, and a deep resonant voice. Was a booming voice a requirement to be a sea captain? He started his career as a young able seaman in 1966, became captain in 1988 and had sailed to ports all around the world. His latest tour was from the Baltic Sea to Genoa, Italy.

The next morning I dreamed I was outside in bright sunshine, but couldn't open my eyes. I tried and tried, and when they finally opened, bright sunshine was streaming through the porthole and onto my face. Temperatures forecast for Sydney were 29C, about lower 80s F. The Sydney skyline, on the port side was in the distance. Captain Peter had already told us that we would not sail grandly under the Sydney Harbor Bridge, as I had fantasized. It became obvious later that the bridge was not high enough or the harbor large enough to accommodate commercial ships.

When Captain Cook first landed in a calm harbor on Australia's southeastern coast, he found such an abundance of unfamiliar plants that he stayed there nine days collecting and preserving specimens, naming the harbor, Botany Bay. British government officials were so impressed by his description that they decided this would be an ideal location for their convict population. In 1787, they sent out their first shipment of 736 unlucky individuals. Cook had landed at Botany Bay in rainy autumn; the convict ships landed in summer, revealing parched earth unable to sustain a colony. The ships sailed north to Cook's second stop, a harbor that he named Port Jackson. Great Britain ultimately emptied 160,000 convicts from their prisons, sending them to survive, if they could, without the aid of the Mother Country. They did survive and Port Jackson became present day Sydney, the most identifiable port in the Southern Hemisphere.

During succeeding centuries, the original Botany Bay became home to what Sydney did not want—commercial docks, the airport, oil refineries, and industries belching smoke. It was called "the septic tank of Sydney." To make matters worse, sand-mining companies dug below sea level, extracting sand for construction and filling the holes with demolition waste. Perhaps that explained the problem expressed by the boat pilot on our way into the harbor. "Australia has had a water shortage for the last seven years. We can't drill for underground water in Sydney," he said. "The underground water is salt water, so we must rely on rainfall and strict water conservation."

The captain permitted us to stand on the bridge and watch our entrance into Botany Bay. It is a protected harbor, guarded by two large bluffs with waves eroding the rocks at tide level. The sea was blue green. Brightly colored planes were landing on the airport runways, which began at water level. With green grass and darker green trees on the hillsides, it didn't look as disagreeable as its occupants might indicate. Nevertheless, puffs of smoke indicated that this was a site of heavy industry. The Sydney skyline was outlined faintly in the distance, about twenty-five kilometers away.

Bill took the distance reading on his GPS; we were 7491 miles from Long Beach. Half our trip was completed. When we finally returned to California, we discovered our round trip had been eighteen thousand miles. First Officer Thomas saw Bill looking at his GPS and said, "What's that?" He had not seen an individual GPS before. He and Bill checked the personal GPS and the ship's GPS readings and found that there was only eighteen feet discrepancy between the two!

Checking the GPS

CHAPTER 11
Sydney

Than told us that the Seafarers' Mission in Sydney provided a shuttle van for transporting seamen from their ships to downtown Sydney. Because we were listed on the ship's manifest, we were able to use this service, saving a huge cab fare. The van followed a regularly scheduled route between the docks and the mission, which was located on Sussex Street. We waited for the van in the heat while swatting big, black flies from our faces. Once we arrived downtown, we changed money at the Seafarers' Mission and walked to Haymarket and Paddington's, both famous for shopping. Haymarket is a giant shopping mall, covering three levels with food courts on every floor and retail shops selling everything from Chinese kimonos to American jeans. A large cinema and Chinese restaurant were located on the third level.

Paddington's was located in the basement. It resembled a giant flea market with clothing, flowers, Cuban cigars, fruits, and vegetables. It was interesting to see but had nothing we wanted, although we frequently heard the comment, "You want to buy something? Go to Paddington's."

Just across the street was the entrance to Chinatown, identified by a large bright red-and-gold arch. Gold stars were strung from lampposts to celebrate the approach of Christmas. Lots of people were milling around. We had to remember to walk on the left side of the sidewalk and to look left when crossing the street. I wondered how many Westerners had forgotten that rule and accidentally stepped in front of a car. And so many restaurants—each one with a menu board and an employee hawking their special menus. Finally, we gave in to requests from a middle-aged woman and ate oyster beef and shrimp with fried noodles.

It was a short walk back to the mission. Volunteers here were not as friendly as in Melbourne, but services were essentially the same: phones, Internet, a large TV showing CNN world news, worldwide newspapers, magazines, souvenirs, and snacks. Stella Maris missions provide a valuable service to seamen: a place to hang out and relax, communicate with families at home, and transportation to and from their ships, all at no cost because the missions are supported by the Anglican Church.

The next morning, we said good-bye to Captain Peter and First Officer Thomas, thanking them for their kindness. We had already told Mr. Odefey how much we liked the crew. He said, "They'll definitely have another job with our company."

The first shuttle bus left at 9:35 a.m. We hurried to the security gate and found that we were the only passengers on an early Sunday morning. Officer Thomas had told us to catch the red Explorer bus when we arrived in the city. This bus, similar to the city tram in Melbourne, stopped at or near the city's attractions and provided a recorded narrative of each one. The difference was that the tour lasted for two and a half hours in Sydney and cost thirty-six dollars per person for a one-day ticket. However, passengers could hop on and off the bus at will for an entire day.

This was the best way to see the city, and we sat through the entire tour before deciding where we wanted to spend the most time. The bus traveled from Chinatown to the Rocks (the site of the first settlement) to the bohemian area around King's Cross, past Hyde Park (the site of the first racetrack), with a brief photo stop at Sydney Harbor and the Opera House, through the downtown financial district, and across the harbor to the new financial center in South Sydney. We had a bird's-eye view and knew where we wanted to spend the remaining hours.

Our first stop was number twenty, Darling Harbor. We walked across Pyrmont Bridge, a walking bridge dividing Cockle Bay and Darling Harbor. What a view! Ahead of us was the skyline of Sydney—the harbor on either side of the bridge, flags fluttering in the wind, restaurants lining the shore, and boats! Sailboats and powerboats, cruise boats too, were constantly coming and going. We ate fish and chips and watched families eating together and enjoying the warm sun. I thought, "What a wonderful way to spend Sunday afternoon."

Darling Harbor

The aquarium was located a little further down the dock, and we decided to go there and see examples of marine life from all over Australia. The first exhibit was of small penguins sometimes seen in Sydney Harbor, looking like ducks above the water and fish under the water. Most visitors, particularly the children, liked the shark display. The exhibit was constructed so that as we walked through, we saw sharks, manta rays, stingrays, and other large, ugly fish swimming over, under, and beside us. It was a little startling to look up and see a shark overhead, his sharp teeth pointed down. The fins we saw showing above the water resembled a fin we saw one day in the wake of the ship.

An outstanding display was of the colorful fish found on the Great Barrier Reef. Each tank showed schools of brightly colored fish with stripes and dots, more combinations than I can remember. In another tank was a banana eel—it really did resemble a very long piece of banana peel that might have been thrown in the trash. Finally, the crocodile display—I didn't know the difference between a crocodile and an alligator, but I learned there. The difference is that the croc displays both upper and lower teeth with its mouth closed. That seems to make the crocodile look a little more ferocious than the alligator.

The next bus stop was the Sydney Opera House. The first surprise was that the roof was not snow white as it appeared in pictures. It was a creamy color, its texture provided by alternating geometric patterns of ceramic tiles.

The wings contained restaurants and bars; the performance area was located in the middle, facing the harbor. It was not possible to tour the hall as a performance was just ending and people were pouring outside, down the steps and into the streets—and inside, down the steps to an underground parking garage. Engineer Zoryan told me that Julio Iglesias was performing the week we were in Sydney; how I wished that I could have heard him.

Close-up of roof

    The second surprise was that Sydney Harbor was not as large as I had expected. It was filled with tourist cruise boats, sailboats, and private powerboats, crisscrossing each other's wakes and narrowly avoiding collisions. Sydney Harbor Bridge loomed just ahead (locals call it the Hangar). On the opposite shore were houses, topped with ochre-colored tile roofs. Reddish-orange, white, and green colors dominated the landscape overlooking the blue-green harbor water.

Sunny Sunday in Sydney

Then we were back on the bus with a trip to the opposite side of the harbor via tunnel. A Japanese consortium completed the tunnel in 1999, taking no immediate payment—only tolls for the next thirty years. The tunnel opened development on the opposite side of the harbor, and South Sydney was now a large financial center. Skyscrapers had names—Zurich, Ing, Telestone, and others—on their sides. A turn right, then left, and the bus was crossing the Sydney Harbor Bridge. The opera house was on the left, the busy harbor was below, and the Sydney skyline was straight ahead. I sighed. I never dreamed that I would ever see this.

Bridge and opera house

We completed our tour driving down George Street and passing the Queen Victoria Building, described as the most beautiful shopping center in the world. Just to the south of the building sat a large bronze statue of an old Queen Victoria holding her scepter. Our day in Sydney had passed, and there was so much more to see…I consoled myself by thinking, "Perhaps on the next trip."

A different shuttle driver took us back to the ship. He took a scenic detour, more attractive than the route we had taken into the city. The driver wanted to show us a dramatic-arts theater donated to Sydney by the actor Mel Gibson. The driver talked fast, drove fast, and frequently turned to look at us while steering with one hand, a behavior I found very disconcerting.

The Hangar

After we arrived at the main gate, he shook our hands, wished us a safe journey, and drove away. We presented our identification, and the security guard looked puzzled as he read his manifest list and said, "The *Tui* is not here. It moved to the opposite dock this afternoon." Panic. How could we get to the other dock? What if the *Tui* had already sailed? We knew that when the ship was ready to sail, it didn't wait for passengers or crew.

The guard phoned the shuttle driver and was able to catch him before he drove too far. He returned and took us to the dock where we had earlier left two Russian seamen, their container ship now docked behind the *Tui*. We breathed a sigh of relief after several moments of anxiety.

Security in New Zealand and Australia was stricter than in the United States. Our ID was checked leaving and entering the dock security gate as well as the main gate. Personnel at all gates had a manifest listing the names and duties of all aboard the ships. They seemed to know where everyone was at all times. We even received the same scrutiny when we left the ship for a day in Ensenada. This contrasted sharply with our experience at Long Beach. There, when we arrived and when we left the ship and dock area, no one requested our identification.

CHAPTER 12
Change of Crew

On November 15, there was a change of crew. Our new captain was German, the officers were Polish, Ukrainian, and Romanian, and the working crew was Filipino. The Polish first officer, Zbigniew Wyludek, said we could call him "Ziggy." (We were so thankful for that concession although some of the officers were surprised that he allowed a nickname.) He was fiftyish, stout, a take-charge person who spoke English that was easy to understand. He had sailed with Captain Behr before and in two days had the ship's operation organized and running smoothly. He posted the days and times when officers and guests could use the washer and dryer. It was no longer necessary to race to the laundry room and hope the washer would be available. The only problem he couldn't fix was the bland taste of the food prepared by the Filipino cook. That became a topic of jokes and some grumbling on the way back to California.

I asked what happened to the extra snacks that we had on the way to Australia, but no one seemed to know. The previous cook had proudly shown off the storage area and cooler stacked with boxes and packages of food, but what had happened to the food? I think the new cook did not know how to cook the items he found. Maybe he never opened the stores to see what was inside.

He frequently served boiled potatoes minus butter or any seasonings. Perhaps he thought a German captain would prefer potatoes at every meal. One day at lunch, the new steward was standing by the table with his hands in his pockets. Captain Behr said, "Percival, get your hands out of your pockets and bring the food." He turned to us. "Those two will not sail with us again when we get back to Australia."

The ship would be in Sydney one more day, and at breakfast, Captain Behr asked if we were going ashore. He was unsure of our departure time. Remembering our panic at the gate the day before and the absence of Australian dollars in our pockets, we opted to stay on board. The captain unlocked the inside doors, giving us access to the air-conditioned bridge and the outside deck by the bridge so that we could watch the loading activities.

Tall cranes in Sydney

As I was standing outside enjoying the sunshine, a crane lifted a container, passed it by me at eye level, and deposited it in the hold.

One of the last containers loaded contained six horses being transported to Tauranga. These horses were located in the same area on the main deck as the previous horses had been, but these were luckier—their stalls faced the sea. They could look out and sniff the fresh salt air. Attending them was a groom named Christopher, who had already made thirty trips this year between Australia and New Zealand. He said it was easier on the horses to travel by plane but cheaper to travel by ship. Two of the horses were Hanoverian, one a stud and one a racer. I don't think the crew enjoyed having the horses on board. Because the horses were stabled on the main deck, it was easy for the crew to hose the straw and manure straight into the sea, but one disgruntled seaman said, "Shit everywhere."

Chris had lived in New Zealand all his life and loved working with horses and fishing for relaxation. He was the third Kiwi we had talked to for an extended period of time, and it was becoming easier to understand his accent. He recommended that we watch the movie *The Whale Rider*, which was available in the ship's library. It was a story about the Maori people and the legend of their arrival in New Zealand on the back of a whale. The Maoris were having the same problems of indigenous people everywhere: unemployment, alcohol abuse, and crime.

The *Tui* was not completely loaded until early on the sixteenth. I had been writing and had not noticed any movement. Bill yelled and reminded me to go to the bridge and watch the departure. The ship had just left the dock and was in the shipping lane, which turned sharply to the left. Two pilots were on board; one was updating his certification, and the other was observing him. The pilot told Bill that he loved the sea and couldn't possibly sit in an office all day. Working as a harbor pilot provided him the opportunity to be at sea and also to be at home with his family.

Sydney pilot boat

    Harbor pilots are trained to know the safest route into the harbor and to be aware of tidal changes, shallow waters, and eroding sandbars. Also, they must be in good physical condition so that they can jump from the pilot boat in rolling waters and climb up the ship's rope ladder. "Pilot on board," the captain would confirm after the deck officer radioed that the pilot was safely on deck. The ship slowed again to allow the pilot to leap to his boat. We looked at the receding hills and the skyline of Sydney, saying good-bye to Australia and hoping to return another day.

CHAPTER 13

WDFIs

ALTHOUGH WE HAD BEEN WARNED that the Tasman Sea between New Zealand and Australia was frequently rough, the three-day voyage to Tauranga couldn't have been better. The sky was sunny; the sea was gentle. Captain Behr opened the passageway doors on our deck, allowing warm breezes to rush through. We sat on the deck, our skin turning more golden each day. About eighty miles from Tauranga, we began seeing the outlines of pointy little islands and rounded islands, as well as dozens of commercial fishing boats with their long nets strung behind them. As the ship moved closer to Tauranga, we noticed private boats were dotted here and there, some anchored in rows, and some even spilling over into the shipping lanes.

One boat was anchored directly in front of the *Tui*, and the owner refused to move. Chris (the new groom) joined us on the bridge. He said, "That guy's not going to move; he has twenty-five to thirty feet of fishing line out." Chris was right. The captain blasted the horn, but the fishing boat did not move. The *Tui* never wavered and passed a few feet to the starboard side of the fishing boat. It was hard to imagine that the fisherman stayed there with a twenty-six-thousand-ton vessel bearing down on him, but he had probably done it before. The captain swore at these little boat owners, calling them WDFIs—wind-driven f***ing idiots. Both Captain Behr and Captain Peter said that small-boat owners don't realize that a large ship cannot make a sudden turn to avoid a collision.

We approached Mount Maunganui, and I'll never forget the beauty of those moments. The sun was behind us, making all the colors vibrant and intense. The waters changed from dark blue to turquoise as we followed the marker buoys located to the right of Mount Maunganui. At the edge of a small swimming beach was a bronze statue of a small boy playing in the water. Visible through the trees were hiking trails going to the top of the mountain. On the left was a huge sawmill with stacks of logs and sawdust, lumber being one of the prime industries of New Zealand.

Marker buoy by Mount Manganui

Shortly after lunch, we were cleared to go ashore. The customs officers were just wrapping up their inspections. "Would you like a ride to town?" they asked. "Just a minute until we clear out the backseat," the taller man said, placing books and briefcases on top of golf clubs in the trunk. The *Tui* was the only ship in port, and no other was expected that day. They were free to spend a Friday afternoon enjoying the spring air—and maybe a round of golf?

We returned to the Strand and the downtown intersection that we had visited two weeks before. The sun was brighter, and the air was warmer. Our objectives were to buy gifts for the family, find a New Zealand wool sweater for Bill, and supply ourselves with snacks to supplement the new cook's bland food. A final objective was to eat dinner on the Strand, enjoy the weather, and watch people.

A clerk at the food market recommended that we eat at the Amphora, an Italian restaurant. Waiters were preparing for a busy evening, setting out tables and chairs and overhead heaters on the sidewalk. I ordered the fish of the day: terakihi, mild with firm white meat and topped with a hollandaise sauce. On our final stroll down the Strand, it seemed that the majority of Tauranga residents were flocking to the harbor restaurants for a glass of wine or a bottle of Fosters. The crowd grew larger as the evening grew longer. There was a spirit of conviviality, sprinkled with conversation, laughter, and the clink of glasses. We hailed a taxi to take us back to the ship and saw our engineer friends waiting at the dock gate. They were planning a night on the town. Bill gave Chief Engineer Misha our last New Zealand dollar and said, "Use it to pay the taxi driver and have a good time." Apparently they did; they didn't return to the ship until 2:00 a.m.

When we left Tauranga the next morning, it was low tide. A very large sandbar was visible on the port side; buoys carefully marked the boating lanes away from it. It was Saturday morning. Kiwis were out for their day in the sun. Small boats were everywhere—in front, beside, following, putting on power to cut in front of us. WDFIs again!

The captain swore loudly. The bright sun, reflecting white and silver on the water, made it hard to see the boats, which were as thick as gnats on a summer evening. After several anxious moments, the boats thinned out a few miles out of the harbor, and soon we were out of sight of land, headed for California, two weeks away.

The water continued to be very calm; it was great weather for sitting on deck. One evening we saw a pink-and-blue sunset. The sea really did resemble glass, it was so smooth. No clear horizon line was evident, and the blue-gray of the water faded into the sky. As the sun continued to go down, clouds appeared low on the horizon. Then the sea turned silver, clouds above were shaded blue, and above that, they were rose colored. When the sun set, a pink tinge came over the silver water. I thought, "I've never seen pink water before." If an artist had painted the sunset, I would have thought he was painting a surreal picture. There were many more beautiful sunsets, each one different. We sat on deck, sipping wine and watching that large orange ball drop from sight. Each evening, the image would change—peach, orange, yellow, mauve, purple, and so many shades of blues and grays. So many colors to remember.

CHAPTER 14

On the Way Home

THE WEATHER ON THE RETURN trip was much the same as on the outbound trip—beautiful sunny weather and gentle seas in the southern latitudes, occasional showers around the muggy tropical equator, wind and storms in the Northern Hemisphere.

A few days north of the equator, we noticed gray skies and increasing wind. Visibility decreased so that it was impossible to distinguish the horizon. White caps grew in size until they looked like constant foam. The ship would pitch sideways and then arch backward and fall forward with a bang. It felt like riding a bucking bronco and a twisting wild bull at the same time. It was obvious why there were side rails on our bed; we had to hold on to keep from falling out. Obviously, we couldn't walk around the ship, or even our cabin, for fear of falling. When we went to the officers' mess, we all held our plates so they wouldn't fall on the deck. After a day and night of Beaufort force-ten winds, I felt angry at the sea. I wanted it to STOP bouncing and bucking. Fortunately, Bill and I are seldom seasick, and we survived this storm without having queasy stomachs.

Not only are high-force winds dangerous for the ship and crew, but they also create precarious conditions for the containers. Apparently the high winds can cause connections to fail, and containers can be swept into the sea. Captain Behr said he once lost 430 containers during a storm in the North Atlantic. I thought about the value of a container and its contents and realized what a financial loss this would be.

Daily routine was the same with occasional splashes of humor, usually at the cook's expense. One day at lunch, we had cabbage soup. Captain Behr lifted a long ribbon of dark green, which might have been an outer cabbage leaf, and said, "Where did this come from—the sea?" It did resemble seaweed. Because many of the dishes had the same flavor, everyone started saying, "The food is the same—only the name is different." Conversations centered on our favorite foods from home and how to cook them. Engineer Misha told us about a favorite food from Russia—some kind of hot (in temperature) meatball that was followed by a shot of ice-cold vodka. Ziggy described a Polish stew with pork and sauerkraut, and the captain pursed his lips in memory of herring from the Baltic.

Dinner with Captain Peter and officers

We learned more about the crew during our two-week return voyage. Chief Engineer Zoroyan (his nickname was Misha—Mike in English) was over six feet tall with an olive complexion and black hair. He seemed unwilling to speak to us initially, but later, he explained that was because his English was poor. Although he was from Ukraine, he grew up speaking Russian. He surprised me when he asked, "What are your roots?" I thought he meant "routes" and was asking how we got to the ship. He said, "No, in America, everyone came from another country. Where did you come from?" After I explained our family genealogies, he said that his father was Ukrainian, and his mother was Armenian. We talked about the displacement of Armenians and why so many of them live outside their native country.

Second Engineer Arndt was a few inches shorter than Misha. He had dark-brown hair and eyes and a mischievous grin that he tried to hide behind his sardonic remarks. One of his first comments was that I said *nostrovia* with a Russian pronunciation rather than Polish. How would I know the difference between Russian and Polish pronunciations? I had only ever heard the word on TV or in a movie. He was Polish with a German surname. He never revealed much about himself except to name all the seaports he had visited on ports of call. When Engineer Misha completed his contract, Engineer Arndt would take over as chief engineer.

The electrician, a Romanian, was also tall with dark hair and gray eyes and full lips that resembled those of a Roman statue. Perhaps I thought that because he said his surname, Pascale, was Italian. He had been going to sea for twelve years and seemed to know a lot about American basketball, cities, and politics. He told us about his daughter, age seven, and his son, age eleven months. His daughter was taking English in school but knew many more words from watching cartoons on TV. In Romania, the cartoons were broadcast in English with no subtitles. That reminded me of the children we had seen in

Hungary, who, like children in the United States, sat in their pajamas watching Saturday-morning cartoons.

I had the pleasure of sitting opposite these good-looking men at the dining table and drinking occasional toasts with them in the evening. Although all of us had problems with comprehension, we were able to compare and contrast our countries. Our questions to them, such as, "Are you able to travel wherever you want now?" may have seemed as strange as their questions to us, such as, "Do you think you are *really* free?"

We tried to learn about each other's cultures. "Where is Ukraine?" "Where is Missouri?" Fingers pointed to locations on the world map posted beside our dining table. "What is the weather like in your country?" "What kinds of food do you eat?" We tried to carefully answer their questions, hoping to erase some stereotypes about Americans.

We saw the two remaining officers very seldom. The second officer was also Romanian, but he seemed unsure of himself and was difficult to engage in conversation. The third officer was Filipino. Bill talked with him during his duty on the bridge, which was fairly often. Officer Elias said it was difficult for Filipinos to obtain positions as officers; those jobs were filled by Eastern Europeans. He had waited several months for this opportunity. He, as well as the Myanmar second and third officers, never ate with us in the officers' dining room. The Filipino crew did not seem as warm and friendly as the Myanmar crew, but the Filipino crew members were new and just learning their jobs.

I learned more about the working crews from talking with volunteers at the Seafarers' Mission and reading the literature available there. The Mission to Seafarers is a world mission agency supported by the Anglican Church, and Her Royal Highness Princess Anne is president. There are personnel present in three hundred ports, while in over a hundred ports, the organization operates seafarers' centers, such as the ones we visited in Melbourne and Sydney. Their newsletter, *Flying Angel News*, highlighted some of the problems faced by seamen and the society's attempts to alleviate them.

New international security regulations in port are making it more difficult for crew members to go ashore. This is particularly true in the United States. When we arrived in San Francisco and Long Beach, none of the crew members were allowed to leave the ship because they had no passports—only a seaman's card. After weeks, sometimes months, at sea, it is important to have even a few hours on shore and time to check on families at home. With larger ships and faster loading times, port stays are shorter, so a seaman can be at sea for several months without having time ashore. It is a lonely life, cut off from family contact. The officers, in contrast, have passports and access to e-mail while on the ship. E-mail is not available to members of the crew.

Even worse conditions may occur when sailing as part of the crew on flags of convenience (FOC) ships. FOCs are often flagged in countries that have little or no maritime infrastructure and little interest in monitoring the physical condition of ships or working conditions on board. If problems are discovered, it is easy for the ship's owners to transfer flags to another FOC country and continue operating as before. Crews pay a heavy price for this. The stories are always the same: a ship in violation of international regulations or in such bad repair that sailing is life threatening, owners who vanish or declare bankruptcy, and a crew left thousands of miles from home with no money, begging and receiving handouts from local dock unions or seafarers' societies. When the crews are lucky enough to be repatriated, they receive no compensation because the ship's salvage value is not enough to pay their back wages. Crews from third-world countries work in these poor conditions because they are looking for a better way to support their families. Than, our steward, said he could make more money in one month on the *Tui* than he could make in five months at home.

I read a story in the newsletter about some Myanmar seamen who had problems receiving their wages. They told their story to a chaplain but were too terrified to have anything done about it because of the potentially severe penalty—they would never be allowed to work on a ship again, completing depriving them of their livelihood. The Myanmar seamen we had a drink with in Melbourne all said they wanted to quit sailing and stay home, and yet that was not an option for them. They would go home, see their families and celebrate, then look for another contract, always hoping that the next ship would offer good working conditions, reasonable pay, and benefits.

CHAPTER 15

An Unexpected Detour

THE SHIP WAS NOT ABLE to unload in Long Beach as we had expected. Because of the stevedore slowdown, some containers were unloaded in San Francisco and some in Ensenada, Mexico. This gave us a day to tour San Francisco—eating clam chowder at one of the dock restaurants and riding those streetcars up and down the hills. When we returned to the ship, we learned that Engineer Misha's wife had boarded. She would complete the next round trip with him before they flew home together at the end of his contract. Helene was petite and bubbly with black hair and sparkling black eyes. She worked as an architect in Kiev; the couple had one young daughter.

The next evening Misha tapped on our door and asked us to come to his cabin for drinks. He brought toast slices from the galley, which he topped with caviar. Three of the four us talked for several hours; unfortunately, Helene was in bed, seasick on that short trip from San Francisco to Ensenada. I wondered how many days she might spend in her bunk if the ship encountered those high-force winds before crossing the equator.

In Ensenada, Misha and Helene shopped for trinkets with Bill and me, as most tourists do, and we ate big, fat lobsters chosen from the tank at the entrance of the restaurant. Helene didn't speak Spanish, but she had no difficulty bargaining with the street vendors. Misha wanted some authentic Mexican tequila, and we helped him buy a bottle representative of the fine tequila from Jalisco.

The next day the ship docked in Long Beach. Our long journey was over. As we walked toward the security gate, Bill heard a voice calling, "Beel! Beel." It was Helene; she hurried to give us last-minute presents: more caviar, a stenciled tablecloth, and a lacquered plaque, all representative of Ukraine. I wished that she had sailed with us earlier. She would have been a companion, full of fun, and I would have learned more about her native city, Kiev. But such is the way of the sea. People are brought together for brief moments and then separated, leaving only enduring memories.

CHAPTER 16

Reflections

WHILE I PACKED OUR BAGS, I reflected on all that I had learned. I had found a book in the ship's library about Captain Cook's discoveries that helped me understand historic and modern-day Australia. Another book, *The Fatal Shore*, described the hardships of the first settlers who were emptied out of England's prisons. The Umberto Eco book telling about early navigators trying to understand longitude and establish the prime meridian helped me relate to the time changes and the lost and found days at the International Date Line.

I had watched the ship's operations from the bridge with the instruments controlling the ship, and I'd been down to the bowels to see the generators and steering mechanisms—even the manual steering wheel below the main deck, to be used in an emergency. I had listened to the officers tell stories about ports—Cape Town, Jakarta, Pusan, Hong Kong—the names falling from their lips as casually as I said St. Louis or Kansas City. I had watched, fascinated, as containers were placed on and taken off the ship. Who determined which container to pick up first and where to place it for easy unloading? How did the arrangement affect the ship's ballast? I never found out that tidbit, but I had learned so much more than I ever anticipated. The days had gone by so quickly that many of those twenty-six books we'd carried aboard in the duffel bag remained unread and were left in the ship's library.

However, the most lasting memories are always of people. The Myanmar crew members—soft spoken, warm, friendly; the German and Polish captains—disciplined and strict but kind and thoughtful; the officers from Poland, Romania, Ukraine—reserved, quiet, not revealing their true thoughts. We shook hands with Captain Behr and First Officer Ziggy on the main deck, saying good-bye to friends we had known only a short time. Third Officer Elias helped me down the gangplank (although it wasn't necessary) and called me "Lady Helen" for the last time. Second Engineer Arndt said, "Now that you have traveled with us, you know how boring it can be." (He had just received word that his wife was filing for divorce.) Chief Engineer Misha said he had once been on a ship for a year, moving through the days like a robot.

These men represented all the men who spend their lives at sea to provide goods we take for granted. For even though the officers have more freedom than the crew members, they all experience the same loneliness, monotony, and danger. It's a way of life that I never thought about while living in the Midwest, and I developed the highest respect for the life of a seaman. Because of our adventures on the *Tui*, I now have a greater appreciation for the steady stream of international commerce, which requires millions of dollars and thousands of work hours to provide consumers with a bottle of Chilean wine, a cotton shirt from Indonesia, or a package of lamb chops from New Zealand.

54 Days on a Container Ship

ABOUT THE AUTHOR

HELEN MURRAY WHITE AND HER husband, Bill, divide their time between a farm in Missouri and a vacation home at Lake Chapala, Mexico. The couple has traveled to all fifty states and to many countries in Europe. One of their earliest travel wishes was to cross the ocean on a working ship. When the opportunity became available, they booked passage on a container ship traveling to Australia and New Zealand. Their experiences are chronicled in this book.

Other books by Helen Murray White are *Watch Out for Topes*, a book about traveling and living in Mexico, and *Butterfield Overland Mail Route: A History of Settlers in Northern Greene County*,–containing genealogies of early settlers and showing the Butterfield route through the family farm.

Printed in Great Britain
by Amazon